※ Smithsonian

THE
ENVIRONMENTAL
MOVEMENT
THEN AND NOW

EARTH DAY 1990   WASHINGTON D.C.

BY REBECCA STEFOFF

CONSULTANTS:
ELLEN NANNEY, LICENSING MANAGER, AND
KEALY GORDON, PRODUCT DEVELOPMENT MANAGER,
SMITHSONIAN INSTITUTION

CAPSTONE PRESS
a capstone imprint

Smithsonian is published by Capstone Press,
1710 Roe Crest Drive, North Mankato, Minnesota 56003
www.mycapstone.com

Library of Congress Cataloging-in-Publication Data
Cataloging-in-publication data is on file with the Library of Congress.
ISBN 978-1-5435-0388-3 (library binding)
ISBN 978-1-5435-0392-0 (paperback)
ISBN 978-1-5435-0396-8 (ebook pdf)

Editorial Credits
Michelle Bisson, editor; Russell Griesmer, designer;
Svetlana Zhurkin, media researcher; Laura Manthe, production specialist

Photo Credits
Alamy: sjbooks, 15; Dreamstime: Yitao Liu, 23; Getty Images: Archive Photos, 9,
Bettmann, 5, 7, 19, 49, 50, CBS Photo Archive, 4; iStockphoto: negaprion, 37; Library
of Congress, 12, 17; Newscom: akg-images, 11, Zuma Press/Santa Cruz Sentinel, 39,
Zuma Press/Terry Herbig, 8; Science Source: Richard T. Nowitz, cover (top right), 1
(bottom); Shutterstock: Andrei Orlov, 57, Brandt Bolding, 31, Christopher Penler, 44,
Joseph Sohm, 42, Kenneth Sponsler, 40, michelmond, 46, Patrick Civello, 32, Serge
Skiba, 20, wavebreakmedia, cover (left), 1 (top); U.S. Fish and Wildlife Service, 26,
35; Wikimedia: U.S. Department of Energy, 54
Design Elements by Capstone and Shutterstock

Printed in the United States of America.
010844S18

TABLE OF CONTENTS

4

Rachel Carson being interviewed about *Silent Spring* for CBS News

In 1962 a biologist named Rachel Carson published a book. The storm it stirred up is still felt today.

Carson's earlier books had been about the sea. The new book was different. It was a warning about pesticides, chemicals used in the United States and around the world to kill insects. That book was *Silent Spring.* One side effect of these chemicals was that they killed birds, or kept them from reproducing. The birdsong of spring mornings could disappear, Carson warned.

Birds weren't the only ones affected. Pesticides could linger in the soil and water. They could harm every living thing in the food chain, including humans. Carson felt that wide use of such chemicals was a huge experiment, with Earth as a laboratory. "For the first time in the history of the world," she wrote, "every human being is now subjected to contact with dangerous chemicals from the moment of conception until death."

A biplane dusted a field with pesticides.

The chemical and agricultural industries loudly opposed *Silent Spring*. They claimed that Carson wanted human beings to return to the Dark Ages, when insects carried diseases that killed vast numbers of people. They pointed out that pesticides such as weed-killers and chemical fertilizers had greatly increased the amount of food grown around the world.

Carson's answer was that people deserved to know about the risks as well as the benefits of such chemicals. In an appearance on the news program *CBS Reports*, she said: "We still talk in terms of conquest. We still haven't become mature enough to think of ourselves as only a tiny part of a vast and incredible universe. I think we're challenged as mankind has never been challenged before, to prove our maturity and our mastery, not of nature, but of ourselves."

Silent Spring helped launch the modern environmental movement. Many people who read Carson's book went on to join that movement. But her book was not the only thing that roused people to action during the 1960s.

SIGNS OF TROUBLE

In 1963 a group of Arizona lawmakers presented a plan for new dams and reservoirs on the Colorado River. One of them, the proposed Bridge Canyon Dam, would be 740 feet high—the tallest dam in the Western Hemisphere at that time. The National Park Service warned that it could flood the Grand Canyon. The Sierra Club was also alarmed.

The Sierra Club had been created in California in May 1892 with three purposes. Two of them were "to explore, enjoy, and render accessible the mountain regions of the Pacific

Coast" and "to publish authentic information concerning them." The third purpose was "to enlist the support and cooperation of the people and government in preserving the forests and other natural features of the Sierra Nevada."

By the 1960s the Sierra Club had become a protector of the larger environment. It fought the planned Bridge Canyon Dam with newspaper ads. One ad said, "Now Only You Can Stop the Grand Canyon From Being Flooded . . . For Profit."

Americans were fired up by such ads. They urged Congress to block the dam. In 1968 Congress passed a plan for Arizona water management that did not include the Bridge Canyon Dam.

A different crisis unfolded in 1968, on the other side of the United States. During a nine-day strike by New York City's garbage collectors, 100,000 tons of garbage and trash built up on the city's streets.

A woman walked through mounds of garbage to reach the mailbox.

" Garbage was piled chest-high," said one account. **Egg shells, coffee grounds, milk cartons, orange rinds, and empty beer cans littered the sidewalk. "**

The garbage was removed when the strike ended. Still, it was a disturbing reminder of how much garbage the city produced—garbage that had to go somewhere.

The year 1969 brought two environmental disasters on the water. In Cleveland, Ohio, flames rose from the Cuyahoga River. Oil and other chemicals spewed into the river by various industries burned for half an hour. Pollution in that river had caught fire before, in 1952, and had burned for two days. Then, off the coast of Santa Barbara, California, an oil-drilling platform had an equipment failure.

Workers spread straw on oil-covered waters after the Santa Barbara oil spill.

More than 3 million gallons of oil leaked into the Pacific Ocean. A shocked nation saw newspaper pictures of oil-covered birds, dead seals and dolphins, and 35 miles of black, sticky coastline.

The 1969 Santa Barbara oil spill was the worst in U.S. history at the time—and for 20 years afterward. The *Los Angeles Times* has called it the "birth of the modern environmental movement." That movement was part of the wind of change that blew through society in the 1960s.

A TIME OF CHANGE

A lot of children were born after World War II. They came of age in the 1960s. This large population of young people came to be called the Baby Boomers. They created a youth counterculture with its own new music, hairstyles, and clothing.

THE FIRST EARTH DAY

Students around the United States were busy on April 22, 1970. In New York, fourth graders cleaned a Manhattan park, and high school students cleared litter from a beach in Brooklyn. Similar events occurred in other cities and towns.

These actions were part of the nation's first Earth Day. The idea started with Gaylord Nelson, a senator from Wisconsin. Nelson had seen the 1969 oil spill that had damaged 35 miles of the California coast. He called for a "national teach-in on the environment." Nelson and other organizers set the date for what came to be called Earth Day. They invited people and groups to take part. According to *Time* magazine, 20 million people accepted that invitation.

Earth Day was "an astonishing grass-roots explosion," Nelson said. "The people cared and Earth Day became the first opportunity they ever had to join in a nationwide demonstration and send a big message to the politicians—a message to tell them to wake up and *do* something."

Many of them questioned the "business as usual" model of American life. They wanted to change things. A mood of unrest, protest, and reform swept the country.

The counterculture had its dark side. Drug use became a problem. Violence erupted at some protest marches and demonstrations. But many young people became activists because they believed they could make society better. They joined the civil rights movement and the women's movement to seek equal treatment for African Americans and for women. They protested against the Vietnam War in southeast Asia because they saw it as unjust. And some of them became environmentalists.

Three things came together in the 1960s to form the modern environmental movement. One thing was the overall atmosphere of social movements and activism. People were marching, waving signs, and forming groups to fight for their causes. Those who felt strongly about nature and the environment drew strength from the hopeful feeling that change was not only possible but on the way.

The crises were the second thing that seized people's attention, from those outlined in *Silent Spring* to the Santa Barbara oil spill. These crises gave people clear goals to fight for—outlawing certain pesticides, for example, or changing the rules for drilling oil at sea. Many people became environmentalists in the 1960s because of specific events.

The third thing was history. Long before the 1960s people had cared about environmental issues, even if they did not use that term. The modern environmental movement drew on the work of those who had gone before.

As a protest against air pollution, these women donned gas masks at a rally.

The environmental movement of the 1960s could be likened to streams flowing into a single river. People joined from different directions. The biggest streams that fed into the movement were conservation and preservation, science, and activism. Each had its source in the past.

THE CONSERVATIONISTS

Conservation and preservation were early forms of environmentalism. Preservation was used in the 19th century, conservation in the 20th. This movement was devoted to protecting natural resources and keeping parts of the country (or the world) wild.

Conservationists believed that individuals and society were better when people could experience nature in places without human activities such as ranching and logging. The conservationists wanted some wilderness areas saved for future generations to enjoy.

Frederick Law Olmstead was an architect. He is best known for designing Central Park in New York City. He was also a conservationist. Olmstead believed that people needed and deserved ways to connect with nature. After he spent time in California's Yosemite Valley, he urged the U.S. Congress to make the valley a nature park for all. In 1864 Congress set Yosemite aside for "public use, resort, and recreation." It was managed first by the state of California and then by the federal government.

Another well-known early conservationist was Theodore Roosevelt. During his presidency, from 1901 to 1909, Roosevelt protected 150 national forests, five national parks, 18 national monuments, 51 federal bird reserves, and four federal game reserves. The National Park Service still calls Roosevelt "the conservationist president."

Artists and writers were part of the conservation movement. Works by painter Thomas Moran and photographer William Henry Jackson showed Americans the mountains, rivers, canyons, and forests of the West. In 1871 Moran and Jackson were part of a government survey of the Yellowstone region. Jackson photographed marvels such as hot springs and waterfalls. His pictures helped persuade Congress to make Yellowstone the country's first national park in 1872.

In 1854 Henry David Thoreau published *Walden; or, Life in the Woods*. It told of two years spent living on the shore of Walden Pond, Massachusetts. *Walden* led later generations of Americans to think about a simple life in nature. In his 1864 book *Man and Nature*, George Perkins Marsh argued that forests and other natural resources must be protected and used with care. Only this way could people and nature remain in balance.

One of the most important of the early conservationists was John Muir of California. A lover of hiking and wilderness, Muir founded the Sierra Club in 1892. He wrote that all living things are connected with each other and the land: "When we try to pick out anything by itself, we find it hitched to everything else in the universe."

During the 1960s Muir's writings found new readers in schools and colleges. His words about nature were often poetic. In *Travels in Alaska* (1915) Muir wrote:

"When we contemplate the whole globe as one great dewdrop, striped and dotted with continents and islands, flying through space with other stars all singing and shining together as one, the whole universe appears as an infinite storm of beauty."

Hunters and anglers (people who fish) also contributed to the conservation movement. They knew that the outdoor activities they loved needed wildlife and places for it to live. People who loved the outdoors formed groups such as the Izaak Walton League. It was founded in 1922 to protect waterways and fish.

During the 1960s conservation broadened to include the entire planet. Americans found themselves uniting

A DUTY TO THE LAND

Aldo Leopold (1887-1948) was a key figure in the American environmental movement. After studying forestry Leopold joined the U.S. Forest Service. His work helped establish the nation's first official wilderness area, the Gila Wilderness in New Mexico. After Leopold moved to Wisconsin, his family replanted trees and prairie plants on an old farm. They then recorded the changes in plants and wildlife that followed.

Leopold's 1949 book, *A Sand County Almanac*, published a year after his death, has inspired many environmentalists. It is a collection of writings about the natural world and the relationship of humans to it. Leopold wrote about what he called "the land ethic," which means that people have a duty to care for the land and the living things that share it. He saw humans as part of a community that includes soil, water, plants, animals, and air. Caring for one means caring for all.

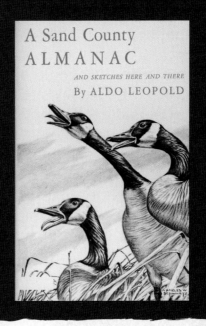

A Sand County ALMANAC
AND SKETCHES HERE AND THERE
By ALDO LEOPOLD

with people from other countries in their concern for tropical rainforests, ocean reefs, endangered African wildlife, and many more things that seemed at risk around the world.

Science was another stream that flowed into the environmental movement. Rachel Carson was just one of many scientists who have written books and articles about the environment.

Paul Ehrlich is a biologist. In 1968 he published an explosive book called *The Population Bomb*. Ehrlich said that the number of people in the world was growing at a rate that would bring disaster in the future. If people did not choose to control population growth, the world faced widespread poverty, hunger, and ecological ruin, he said.

From the start, critics have disagreed with some of Ehrlich's statements and predictions. However, his widely read work added population growth to the list of environmental concerns.

People in the 1960s started to hear and see more about ecology, a science that had emerged around the beginning of the 20th century. It is the study of how living things interact with each other and with their environments. The ecologist sees the natural world as interlocking systems, not separate pieces. Although the word *ecology* was new to many nonscientists, it had been created by German scientist Ernst Haeckel in 1866.

One of the first Americans to write about ecology was a chemist named Ellen Swallow Richards, who began her career in the 1870s. Richards wanted to make people and the environment healthier by applying science to home activities including cooking and cleaning. In the 1880s she wrote about nutrition and the importance of clean air and water.

Richards was also one of the first scientists to test public drinking water for safety. Because of her work, Massachusetts became the first state to set standards for water quality. This kind of activism for public health became a major part of the modern environmental movement.

A leading figure in the movement in the 1960s and 1970s was Barry Commoner. He was a professor of biology who taught an ecological understanding of nature.

His 1971 book, *The Closing Circle*, introduced readers to the principles of ecology. It also spread the idea of sustainability, which is using natural resources without using them up, and with as little damage as possible to the environment.

Ellen Swallow Richards

PUTTING PASSIONS INTO ACTION

These streams made the modern environmental movement broad enough to hold people with various points of view and goals. The movement included children, teens, and young adults. Scientists, hippies, and politicians who cared about "green" or environmental issues all had roles.

New organizations sprang up, including the League of Conservation Voters (1969), Friends of the Earth (1969), and Greenpeace (1971). Older organizations, such as the Sierra Club and the National Audubon Society, gained new members and a new sense of purpose.

Environmental groups had different paths toward their goals. Some took direct action to save the land or wildlife. Greenpeace, for example, became known for direct actions. Its first mission took place in 1971. Founders of the group sailed a small ship toward the island of Amchitka, Alaska, to protest the U.S. government's testing of nuclear weapons. These weapons do lasting harm to air, sea, soil, and living things. Bad weather and the U.S. Navy kept the Greenpeace ship from reaching the island. But newspapers reported on the mission. The government was criticized and stopped testing at Amchitka.

Another kind of direct action was carried out by the Nature Conservancy. It grew out of a group founded in 1915 to publish ecological studies of North and Central America. By the 1940s some members also wanted to save natural places. In 1951 they took the name Nature Conservancy. Four years later the group made its first land purchase. It bought 60 acres along a river valley in New England.

The Nature Conservancy pioneered something called conservation easements in the 1960s. This is a legal agreement that lets owners of land keep their property with the conservancy setting rules for protecting it. Through easements, purchases, and partnerships with governments and parks, the conservancy has directly protected many important ecosystems.

Other environmental groups took a political approach. The League of Conservation Voters was created to be a link between politics and people who care about the environment. The league keeps track of how politicians vote and act on

Members of Greenpeace near the ship they sailed to
Alaska to protest nuclear weapons testing.

environmental issues. It provides that information to the public, and it supports environment-friendly politicians.

Friends of the Earth began by protesting against nuclear energy programs in the United States. After a few years it became an international network of environmental groups in many countries. They share a belief in sustainable development and environmental justice.

All of the social movements of the 1960s built upon the struggles and victories of earlier decades. But they won new victories during the 1960s. After years of protests against unequal treatment of African Americans and other minorities, the U.S. Congress passed the Civil Rights Act in 1964. At the end of the 1960s, after years of protests by the antiwar movement, the United States slowly began to bring troops home from the Vietnam War.

What about the environmental movement? What results did it produce?

The Shining Rock Wilderness is a protected area in North Carolina.

CHAPTER 3

TO SAVE THE PLANET

Environmentalism touched more lives as the 1960s went on. Children did school projects on topics such as recycling and solar power. Grandparents joined college students in protests outside the offices of chemical companies.

The environmental motto "think globally, act locally" summed up the double nature of the movement. Some problems, such as air pollution, were spread over wide areas—even the whole world. Environmentalists wanted people to think about the global scale of these issues. They also wanted people to take action in their own communities against local problems.

Even small actions like cleaning trash out of a stream could help.

Green groups swelled with new members. They also joined forces to work together on many issues. These environmental organizations pressured Congress to pass new laws. In addition, they went to court to enforce laws that already existed or to challenge the way land was being used.

One by one, the movement won legal victories.

VICTORIES OF THE 1960S

The U.S. Congress passed some major federal environmental laws in the 1960s. They began a wave of

NUCLEAR PROMISE AND PERIL

Nuclear power shows that even within a movement, people may disagree.

The United States ended World War II by dropping nuclear bombs on Japan in 1945. In the years that followed the shadow of nuclear war loomed over the world. The Soviet Union and the United States built stockpiles of nuclear weapons. By 1967 the United Kingdom, France, China, and Israel also had such weapons.

At the same time, scientists were harnessing nuclear forces to produce electricity. Nuclear power promised to meet the growing need for energy without burning fossil fuels such as coal and oil. By the late 1950s nuclear power plants were in use in the Soviet Union, the United Kingdom, and the United States. In early 2017 the world had more than 440 commercial nuclear power reactors. Some older nuclear plants have been closed, but new ones are being built.

Many environmentalists are against the use of nuclear power. They point out two problems. One is the risk of disasters. The other is waste material. Nuclear waste gives off harmful radiation for many years after it is no longer used to make energy.

Disasters have occurred at nuclear power plants. Three of the most serious were at Three Mile Island, Pennsylvania, in 1979; at Chernobyl, Ukraine, in 1986; and at Fukushima, Japan, in 2011. And the problem of nuclear waste keeps growing. Many power plants now store much more radioactive waste than they were built to hold. The United States has not yet found a place for safe, long-term storage of the hazardous material that could poison soil, water, and air.

Some environmentalists have supported nuclear energy. One of them is Patrick Moore, a former leading figure with Greenpeace. Another is James Lovelock, who researched air pollution for NASA. They claim that with better technology and safety rules, nuclear power plants would be better for the environment than fossil fuels.

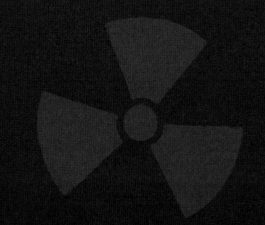

lawmaking that would continue into the next decade.

In the early 1960s conservation groups pressured Congress to pass a bill that would protect some wild areas from development. The American people strongly supported it too. By 1962 letters to Congress in favor of the wilderness bill outnumbered letters about any other bill.

In 1964 the Wilderness Act became law. It set aside 54 areas of federal land to be named wilderness. It also established the legal definition of

The disaster at the Three Mile Island nuclear power plant was a wake-up call to many Americans.

wilderness as "an area where the earth and its community of life are untrammeled by man, where man himself is a visitor who does not remain."

In the eyes of conservationists, the Wilderness Act did not go far enough. Lawmakers had also felt pressure from mining and electric companies that did not want to see large amounts of land sitting unused. The law allowed mining in wilderness areas. It also allowed the president to authorize dams and power plants in them. And it protected only 9.1 million acres, not the 60 million hoped for by conservationists.

But the Wilderness Act was an important first step. More wilderness areas were added later. Within 25 years the national wilderness system held 474 units—more than 90 million acres in all.

Conservation groups and the public fought the plan to build a dam near the Grand Canyon. They won that fight. Their success led to the National Wild and Scenic Rivers Act of 1968. The act protected eight rivers in their natural and free-flowing states. As with the Wilderness Act, more rivers were later added. As of 2014 the act protected nearly 13,000 miles of 208 rivers in 40 states and Puerto Rico.

In 1969 Congress passed what environmentalist Kirkpatrick Sale called the "act that was to be the most influential of all." This was the National Environmental Policy Act (NEPA). The pressure that led Congress to pass this act came from *Silent Spring*, from the Santa Barbara oil spill, and from a decade of rising alarm about the environment. President Richard Nixon signed NEPA into law on the first day of 1970.

NEPA applied to any government agency that planned a new law or project. First the agency had to find out how the law or project would affect the environment. This report would be called an environmental impact statement.

To do the huge job of overseeing environmental policy, NEPA created a new federal office called the Environmental Protection Agency. The EPA would also monitor how well the country followed federal environmental laws—including several major laws passed in the 1970s.

THE GREEN LAWS OF THE 1970s

Congress had passed the Water Pollution Control Act in 1948. It was the first step toward limiting the amount of sewage and waste that communities and industries could dump into the nation's waters. In 1955 Congress passed the Air Pollution Control Act. It gave states the responsibility for controlling the chemicals, soot, and ash that were polluting the air.

In the early 1970s, with environmental awareness at a new high, both acts were made much stronger.

The Clean Air Act of 1970 called for strict regulations on fixed sources of air pollution, such as factories, and also on moving sources, such as cars and trucks. Automakers fought to block the act because it forced them to add new pollution-reducing technology to vehicles.

The Clean Air Act marked the beginning of improved air quality in American cities. The 1970 act was "a huge change in the law," California environmental professor and reporter Larry Pryor later said. "[C]ompared to

A biologist collected a sample from a male yearling wolf to help conservation efforts.

where we were in 1970, the regulators have done a miraculous job holding down air pollutants."

The 1969 fire on the Cuyahoga River in Ohio led to calls for tighter limits on waste in the waterways. In 1972 Congress passed a sweeping update of the nation's water pollution law. The new version is generally known as the Clean Water Act. Among other things, it set new standards for testing drinking water, for releasing material into waterways, and for monitoring pollution.

Another important new law was the Federal Insecticide, Rodenticide, and Fungicide Act of 1972. It controlled the use of pesticides such as those Rachel Carson had described in *Silent Spring*. That same year Congress passed the Marine Mammals Protection Act, which supported conservation of whales, dolphins, and seals.

The Endangered Species Act (ESA) of 1973 was, in the words of conservationist and lawyer Michael J. Bean,

> **a turning point in our relationship with other living creatures with which we share the earth.**

The ESA required the government to recognize when a species of plant or animal was threatened with extinction. It gave the government a duty to keep those species from becoming extinct.

The ESA is administered by the U.S. Fish and Wildlife Service. As of 2017, it listed 1,447 species of animals and 945 species of plants as endangered or threatened. Through conservation and protection, species are sometimes de-listed because they are no longer considered endangered or threatened.

THE STORY OF STORM KING

New laws were one way to reach environmental goals, but there were others. A battle that raged over a New York mountain from the early 1960s until 1980 showed the power of "acting locally"—and of lawyers.

Storm King has an elevation of 1,340 feet along the west bank of the Hudson River. In the mid-19th century it was a popular subject for the landscape painters known as the Hudson River School. In the mid-20th century it was a popular destination for hikers. It had forested slopes and broad views from its summit. In 1962 the Consolidated Edison (Con Ed) power company decided that Storm King was also a good place to build a new power plant.

Plans called for removing part of the mountain, building a dam, and installing a hydroelectric plant. Local citizens objected to a scheme that would destroy not just Storm King's natural ecosystems but also the scenic beauty of the area. They formed a grassroots group called the Scenic Hudson Preservation Conference (SHPC) to fight the power company.

Their challenge would be a legal one. The Federal Power Commission (FPC) had granted Con Ed permission to build the plant. It had also said that the SHPC did not have standing—that is, the legal right to challenge its ruling in court.

SHPC members contacted friends, prominent citizens, politicians, and others. They asked for financial support, letters of protest, and legal help.

In fact, the construction of the power plant became a topic of debate in the New York Senate. Senator Thomas J. Mackell, who described himself as a former employee of Con Ed, said that if the plant were approved, it would open the door to similar projects along the Hudson River. And that, he noted, would be a danger to the environment.

Majority Leader Joseph Zaretzki pointed out the dangers of the high-tension wires that would be needed to carry electriciy to and from the Storm King plant. Other senators voiced similar objections.

The SHPC appealed the FPC decision, and in 1965 the 2nd U.S. Circuit Court of Appeals ruled that the SHPC did have standing. The court recognized the group's special interest in Storm King. That interest was related to conservation and recreation but also to aesthetics—the special beauty and historic importance of the place.

That victory was significant. It was the first time a federal court had granted an environmental group the right to sue on aesthetic grounds. But it was only the beginning of the Storm King fight.

After the SHPC was granted standing, the FPC had to hold another round of hearings about the development plan. Con Ed argued that the plant would provide necessary power to New Yorkers. It said that Storm King was the best site. The SHPC argued that the plant would kill fish, among other environmental harms. In 1970 the FPC ruled that Con Ed should be licensed to build the plant.

SHPC now joined forces with New York City, a fishermen's association, and other groups. They filed a formal request for the FPC to reconsider. They also sued the U.S. Army Corps of Engineers to keep rock from the construction site from being dumped into the Hudson.

Alexander Saunders, chairman of the Hudson River Preservation Conference, said, "We are certain there will be grounds which finally will require the word of the Supreme Court." The case dragged on. In 1976 the state attorney general of New York joined the SHPC in asking the FPC to reconsider the license in light of new, stricter environmental protections. They also said that the economic situation had changed since the 1960s, making the plan out of date.

Finally, in 1980, Con Ed gave up its plan for the Storm King plant. It also agreed to kill fewer fish at its other plants and to set up a fund for environmental research on the Hudson River.

Storm King was a landmark of the environmental movement for several reasons. It showed the power of local, grassroots organizing. It established that conservation groups had legal standing to fight for aesthetic protection of the land.

Most importantly, the Storm King battle harnessed the power of lawsuits.

David Sive, who died in 2014, was for many years a leading lawyer for the SHPC. He later became a founder of the Natural Resources Defense Council, which has taken many environmental cases to court. Sive said that:

> **❝ after Storm King, [e]nvironmentalism has used [lawsuits] as no other social movement has before or since. ❞**

Storm King Mountain, on the bank of the Hudson River, has long been loved for its scenic beauty.

The Hetch Hetchy Dam, Yosemite National Park, California, brought water to San Francisco.

John Muir, who founded the Sierra Club, was a key inspiration for the modern environmental movement. Yet Gifford Pinchot has been called the "father" of American conservation. The two men held different views on how people should treat the land—and they promoted their rival visions in public debates. Their disagreement echoes today in the contrasting opinions and beliefs people have about environmental issues.

TWO VIEWS OF CONSERVATION

Muir cherished untouched wilderness. He fought to preserve it for its own sake, as well as for the enjoyment of people who loved it.

Pinchot cared little for the idea of preserving land for the sake of wildness or scenery. He saw the natural world in terms of resources for people to manage and use. The government, not private companies, should be in charge of that management and use. In his 1910 book, *The Fight for Conservation,* Pinchot wrote: "The central thing for which Conservation stands is to make this country the best possible place to live in, both for us and for our descendants. . . . Conservation is the most democratic movement this country has known for a generation.

It holds that people have not only the right, but the duty to control the use of the natural resources, which are the great sources of prosperity. And it regards the absorption of these resources by the special interests, unless their operations are under effective public control, as a moral wrong."

Pinchot trained as a forest manager. In 1905 President Theodore Roosevelt made him the first chief of the U.S. Forest Service, which took control of the national forests. Pinchot set up rules that let timber companies, mining companies, and ranchers—the "special interests"—buy the right to make money from the national forests, but supervised by the Forest Service.

In 1913 Congress allowed San Francisco to build a dam in the Hetch Hetchy Valley of Yosemite National Park. The dam would flood the valley but bring water to those living in San Francisco. Pinchot supported the dam. Muir opposed it because it would destroy the natural beauty, wildlife, and plants of a protected park.

Conflict about national forests continued after the Muir–Pinchot conservation battle. In 1986 it erupted over a shy brown bird called the northern spotted owl. This owl lives in old-growth forests in the Pacific Northwest. To find food and raise its young, it needs cedar, fir, spruce, and hemlock forests that are 150 to 200 years old.

The spotted owl battle pitted scientists and conservationists against timber companies and loggers. The Forest Service and the Fish and Wildlife Service were caught in the middle. The case centered on the Endangered Species Act of 1973.

THE CASE OF THE SPOTTED OWL

The Endangered Species Act became one of America's most controversial environmental laws. Protecting a threatened or endangered species does not just mean that the species cannot be hunted or killed. It also means preserving the "critical habitat" of the species—the place or places it needs in order to live. This made the ESA unpopular with land-use planners, developers, and land-based industries such as logging and ranching.

In 1986 conservationists asked the Fish and Wildlife Service to protect the northern spotted owl under the Endangered Species Act. Researchers showed that the owl was at risk. It was losing its home forests to logging.

Four years later the Fish and Wildlife Service listed the owl as

Northern spotted owl

threatened (at risk of becoming endangered). It also defined areas of critical owl habitat to be preserved.

Protection of the northern spotted owl angered some people. They saw the owl as an excuse to put sections of national forests off-limits for logging. Timber companies argued that people need wood and paper more than they need an owl that few will ever see.

NOT IN MY BACKYARD

Solving a problem may create a new problem. Landfills solve the problem of where to put garbage. Wind farms of tall turbines solve the problem of how to get clean, renewable energy. But suppose you lived in a neighborhood that did not want to see (or smell) a landfill nearby. Or a beach town that didn't want the sea view changed by offshore wind turbines?

That's where NIMBYism comes in. NIMBY stands for "not in my backyard." The term has been used since at least 1980. It applies to people and organizations that block things they fear will endanger their own homes and communities—or change their look or their value. NIMBYism acts through protests, lawsuits, and boycotts of companies or products.

People taking action to defend their communities seems like a good idea. But there is another point of view. Landfills, wind farms, and other controversial developments such as homeless shelters have to go *somewhere*. Often they end up in poor communities that do not have the money and skills to fight them.

In 2000 Robert D. Bullard studied how decisions about developments had been made. He wrote that "[T]he hazardous wastes, garbage dumps, and polluting industries were likely to end up in someone's backyard. But whose backyard? More often than not, these LULUs (locally unwanted land uses) ended up in poor, powerless, black communities rather than in affluent suburbs." Bullard and others have called for environmental justice. Environmentalists, they say, should seek equal treatment for all.

Communities where people worked as loggers, log-truck drivers, or sawmill employees knew that jobs would be lost. Local economies would suffer. People put "Save a Logger, Eat an Owl" bumper stickers on their trucks. Restaurants served "spotted owl soup."

Conservationists argued that the owl was an indicator species. Its well-being was a sign of the overall health of the forest—and the owl was not doing well. The owl and some sections of critical habitat remain protected under the ESA. Still, lawsuits and disputes among the timber industry, conservation groups, and federal agencies have continued.

The owl's numbers have dropped dramatically in forests outside the legally defined critical habitats. The Oregon

An aerial view of a Florida landfill. Landfills
usually end up in poor neighborhoods.

Fish and Wildlife Office says that unprotected owl habitat could disappear completely in 10 to 30 years.

And the spotted owl has a new problem. Larger, more aggressive barred owls have moved from eastern North America into the spotted owl's range. No one knows why. Barred owls kill spotted owls and take their nests. Forest managers and ecologists now look for ways to control barred owls. They think that only about 2,200 breeding pairs of northern spotted owls remain in Oregon, Washington, and Canada.

HOW FAR IS TOO FAR?

During the heat of the spotted owl controversy, some environmentalists climbed old-growth trees, chained themselves to high branches, and stayed for days. Tree-sitting is a form of direct action people take to protect trees. It can keep the trees from being cut while courts decide their fate.

Living in tents and given food by supporters, some tree-sitters have stayed up for long periods. In 2013 a brushfire drove a woman from her tree-sit in Tasmania, Australia. She had spent 15 months in a 400-year-old tree to protest logging.

Spiking is another form of direct action to protect trees. It means driving long nails or rods into trees—not to harm the trees, but to damage logging equipment. The idea began in the 19th century during feuds between loggers. In modern times it was spread by Dave Foreman in his 1985 book, *Ecodefense*.

A few years earlier Foreman had helped start a group called Earth First, which favored direct action to protect the environment. Earth First believed that most conservation and environmental groups did not go far enough. They felt the groups did not act on their beliefs. Direct action would get real results.

In 1987 a young sawmill worker in California was severely injured while cutting a log. His saw blade struck a metal spike and split. Half of the blade sheared through his face.

Foreman had said, "The purpose of tree spiking is not to hurt anybody; it's to keep trees from being cut." After the disastrous accident, though, Earth First changed its mind about tree spiking. Foreman said the practice should stop.

The term ecoterrorism has been used to describe tree spiking and other destructive direct acts such as cutting power lines or setting fire to bulldozers. These extreme acts are nearly always crimes that involve trespass or property destruction.

Ecoterrorist acts have been carried out by a few extreme environmentalists. Many mainstream environmentalists strongly disapprove of them. They also fear that ecoterrorism could harm the whole environmental movement.

A tree-sitting protester is cheered on by the crowd.

The Cuyahoga River is now clean enough for boats to cruise.

What progress has been made on the problems that fired up the environmental movement in the 1960s and 1970s? Have new problems come to light?

Measuring the results of environmental actions tells a story of successes mixed with shortcomings. One particular problem of the 1960s and 1970s, air pollution, has taken on new meaning. It is now understood as part of an issue that concerns the world—climate change, or global warming.

WATER AND WASTE

The Clean Water Act of 1972 was a response to badly polluted waters. It was meant to make American waterways swimmable and fishable without danger to human health. Results have been uneven.

The big concern in 1972 was pollution from sewage plants and from industry. That has been greatly reduced. Today a bigger problem is runoff—water that flows into streams and rivers from city streets and from farmland, carrying pollution with it. Rules have not kept up with that issue. Progress has been made toward limiting water pollution, but more remains to be done.

From the first Earth Day in 1970 to today, environmentalists have pointed to recycling as something that everyone can do. In fact, recycling is a very old habit. People used to reuse wood, cloth, paper, and many other materials. But by the 20th century many people routinely threw worn-out things away along with their garbage.

The environmental movement brought back the idea of reusing metal, glass, paper, and plastic. By 1990 more than 10,000 American communities had public recycling centers or programs. In many cities recyclable materials are now collected in the same way as garbage.

But EPA records show that Americans are not recycling as much as they could. In 2014 the United States

The first step in the recycling of aluminum cans is to get them to a recycling center.

produced about 258 million tons of solid waste. About 89 tons of it—less than 35 percent—was recycled. If it was plant or food waste, it was composted to make soil.

More than 33 million tons of waste were burned to make energy. Electricity from waste may seem like a good idea. But it pollutes the air with greenhouse gases.

The biggest share of the waste, 136 million tons, was dumped in landfills. Cities spent $5 billion on landfill fees in 2013.

Since the mid-1990s the United States has had a recycling rate of around 35 percent. This is much lower than the recycling rates of some other rich, developed countries. Germany, for example, recycled 65 percent of its waste in 2016. South Korea recycled 59 percent, Slovenia 58 percent, and Belgium 55 percent.

AIR AND CLIMATE

Before the Clean Air Act of 1970 some American cities had serious problems with smog. This brownish haze was made up of chemical pollutants, smoke, and fine dust. Exhaust from cars and trucks contributed largely to smog.

Younger Americans have never seen Los Angeles, New York, or Chicago blanketed with heavy smog for weeks on end. Smog has not entirely disappeared, but American air quality has improved.

Since 1990 the EPA has been required to make regular reports on the benefits and costs of the Clean Air Act. The first report covered the years 1970 to 1990. It showed that four leading pollutants in the atmosphere had decreased by amounts ranging from 30 to 50 percent in 20 years.

Millions marched worldwide in the April 2017 March for Science.

That drop in pollution, said the EPA, saved 184,000 Americans each year from dying early because of pollution-related illnesses. The 2011 report said that by 2020, the Clean Air Act will save 230,000 people from early death each year. It will also reduce illnesses and save trillions of dollars of lost work time.

But the air-quality story is not all positive. Even when pollutants are at or below legal levels, air pollution kills thousands of Americans each year. Beyond that, it is warming up the planet.

Climate change has become a leading environmental issue in the 21st century. NASA reports that the planet's average temperature has risen 1.4 degrees Fahrenheit (0.8 degree Celsius) since 1880. Two-thirds of the increase has happened since 1975.

Earth's temperature has gone up and down many times in the planet's history. The great majority of international scientific experts, though, say this rise is different. First, it is happening faster than natural climate changes of the past. Second, it is more than 95 percent likely that most of the current warming is human-caused.

Burning fossil fuels (oil, gas, and coal) adds greenhouse gases to the atmosphere. So does cutting down forests. When the sun heats Earth, these gases prevent the heat from being reflected back into space. The atmosphere and the planet get warmer.

Climate change is expected to bring many other changes. Glaciers and ice caps are melting. Sea levels are already rising. Extreme weather such as typhoons and deadly heat waves may become more common. Tropical diseases will spread.

Not everyone agrees that global warming is a problem. A few scientists, some politicians, and the fossil fuel industry say it is not happening. Others say that even if it is, humans aren't causing it and can't prevent it.

Around 95 percent of climate researchers agree that global warming is happening. Most claim that people can and should take steps to limit its effects. The single biggest step would be to greatly reduce the use of fossil fuels.

If global warming is fought, it must be a global effort. In 2015 representatives from 195 nations signed the Paris Climate Accord.

WHY WORDS MATTER

When people talk or write about the environment, the words they use can make a difference.

Do you feel the same about *climate change* and *global warming*? Many people don't, according to a 2014 study by researchers from Yale and George Mason universities.

The two terms have different meanings. *Global warming* is the rise in the average temperature of Earth's surface since the Industrial Revolution, which began in the late 18th century. *Climate change* is broader. It is a long-term change in Earth's climate—rain, wind, and ocean currents as well as temperature.

The researchers found that scientists are more likely to use *climate change* unless they are talking only about temperature. The American public slightly favors *global warming* when looking for information online. Reporters often use the terms as if they mean the same thing.

To groups within the U.S. population, the two terms have different meanings. For example, people under 48 are more likely to believe in global warming than in climate change. They are also more willing to join a political campaign against it. A large percentage of African Americans and Hispanic Americans rated global warming as worse than climate change. This shows that words have the power to sway people's feelings about environmental issues.

Cars were submerged as a result of Hurricane Harvey in 2017. Many see the rise in the severity of hurricanes as a clear sign of climate change.

They agreed to reduce fossil fuel use and promote climate-friendly energy sources, such as solar power. The goal of the accord is to keep the world's average temperature from rising more than 3.6 degrees F (2 degrees C) above its temperature level in the mid-19th-century.

TOXIC TROUBLE

Many environmental problems are as hard to solve as they are dangerous. The thousands of sites that have been polluted by mines, chemical factories, and other industries are a leading example. Love Canal brought that problem to light.

Love Canal was an old canal in Niagara Falls, New York. For years the city, the army, and chemical companies dumped waste in it. Then it was filled in. Houses and a school were built over it.

In 1974 a woman named Lois Gibbs moved into the neighborhood with her family. Before long, two of her children were mysteriously ill. She discovered that her neighborhood had a high rate of birth defects, cancers, and other diseases. After learning about the old canal, she was sure that toxic chemicals were to blame. They were leaking into the air, the soil, and the water—even into some people's basements.

Gibbs formed a community association to seek help. They tried to get attention from the state, the EPA, and the media. With Love Canal in the national news, President Jimmy Carter declared a state of emergency there in 1978. The federal government paid $17 million to move 900 families away from the toxic neighborhood. Gibbs went on to work with other communities that were worried about toxic sites.

Congress also took action. In 1980 it passed a law aimed at identifying toxic sites and forcing polluters to clean them up. It also established a fund to pay for cleaning when the polluters could not be found or could not pay.

Superfund, as that program is called, keeps a list of toxic sites to be cleaned. As of May 2017 there were 1,336 sites on the list. Another 53 were waiting to be reviewed. Three hundred and ninety-three sites had been removed from the list. The EPA found that no further work was needed at those sites to protect health or the environment.

The Love Canal case alerted the nation to the lurking problem of toxic waste. It also showed that a single determined activist can start a massive change.

At the age of 66, Tim Moriarty had to abandon his home of 35 years because of the discovery of toxic chemicals seeping into his Love Canal home.

Marchers in Warren County, North Carolina, protested against a toxic waste dump in their area.

Earth Day 2000 was much bigger than the first celebration in 1970. Thousands of groups in 184 countries took part in education and activism.

In 2020 Earth Day will be 50 years old. Each year it calls attention to environmental issues. For many people, it is a symbol of the environmental movement. What will that movement look like in the years ahead?

ENVIRONMENTAL JUSTICE

One trend that may increase in the future is the demand for environmental justice. This demand has traditionally come from the civil rights movement.

In recent years, environmentalists have added their voices.

The environmental justice movement was born in the 1970s in Warren County, North Carolina. It was one of North Carolina's poorest counties. Its population was 75 percent African American.

In 1973 a company had dumped 31,000 gallons of a toxic chemical called polychlorinated biphenyl (PCB) along roads in 14 North Carolina counties. The state decided to build a landfill to hold soil contaminated by the toxin. They chose Warren County as the site of the landfill.

People who lived near the site feared that their drinking water would

ARE WE IN A NEW AGE?

What should we call the age in which we live? Timelines of Earth's 4.6-billion-year history are divided into eras, each lasting hundreds of millions of years. Eras are divided into periods, and the periods are divided into epochs. These divisions are based on geological evidence: the makeup of rock layers. They are agreed on by the International Union of Geological Sciences.

According to the IUGS, we live in the Cenozoic era, the Quaternary period, and the Holocene epoch. Holocene means "entirely recent." It began at the end of the last Ice Age, around 12,000 years ago.

But some environmentalists and scientists think Earth has entered a new epoch. In 2000 Paul Crutzen, a chemist, suggested the term *Anthropocene*. It means "new man." The term has caught on as a way of talking about the present age of widespread human changes to the natural world.

Those changes include nuclear testing (which may leave traces in rock), plastic waste (which breaks down into tiny beads that may be preserved in rock), changes in air and ocean chemistry because of pollution, extinction of many species, and climate change.

But in scientific terms, saying that Earth has entered the Anthropocene epoch means that human activity will leave lasting, worldwide evidence in the geological record. Many geologists think there is simply not enough scientific support for such a claim. There is also the question of when the Anthropocene could be said to have started. In the 18th century, at the dawn of the Industrial Revolution? In 1945, at the dawn of the nuclear age?

The IUGS has agreed to consider the possibility of making Anthropocene official. Before that could happen, however, teams of geologists must unearth convincing evidence from many parts of the world. It may be years before the question "what epoch is this?" is answered.

be contaminated. They organized protests, including lying across roads to block the trucks that carried the soil. Members of the civil rights movement joined them. Eventually their cause drew national attention. There were lawsuits, public hearings, and scientific studies.

In 1982 the state agreed not to enlarge the landfill. It also agreed not to regard Warren County as a site for waste disposal. The next year, however, a leak was discovered in the landfill. Not until 2003 did the state begin destroying the PCB.

The Warren County protests drew attention to the fact that poor people and people of color were especially likely to be victims of environmental hazards. A decade later, the case of Flint, Michigan, showed the nation that the problem had not gone away.

Flint is 57 percent African American. More than 41 percent of its citizens live in poverty. The city had been getting its drinking water from Lake Huron since 1967. In 2014 the city's managers switched to getting drinking water from the Flint River, which was known to have been polluted.

Soon disease bacteria were detected in Flint's water. Citizens were told to boil it before drinking or cooking with it. Then a car manufacturer in Flint stopped using city water because it was damaging engine parts. In 2015 the EPA detected high levels of lead in the water, which was causing old lead pipes to corrode.

Citizens and activists sued the city, demanding to return to the earlier water source. The city refused, saying it would cost too much. By 2016 the National Guard was delivering bottled drinking water to the people of Flint. Half a dozen federal agencies were involved in an investigation. Charges were filed against water officials and members of the city and state governments. In 2017 the EPA and the state government announced plans to upgrade Flint's water system.

Like the Warren County protest, the Flint water crisis showed that the environmental movement can do more than fight for wilderness areas, tropical rainforests, and endangered animals. It could evolve to include all members of society and to recognize environmental injustice at home and abroad.

In March 2017 the United States passed an energy milestone. For the first time more than 10 percent of

Nuclear weapon test Bravo on Bikini Atoll, 1954. Nuclear energy is still used to generate power, but is being replaced in many areas by more environmentally friendly power sources.

the country's energy came from wind and solar power. Less than 1 percent had come from those renewable sources in 2000.

The same thing is happening worldwide. In 2016 the U.S. Energy Information Administration reported that renewables (wind, solar, and hydropower) were the world's fastest-growing source of electricity. Solar power was the fastest-growing type of renewable energy, increasing by more than 8 percent a year.

If these trends continue, they may help limit fossil fuel use. This would have a positive effect on air quality and global warming. Renewable energy has become more affordable and profitable. However, its continued growth depends in part on support from governments.

In early 2017 newly elected President Donald Trump changed the U.S. Clean Power Plan to allow increased mining and burning of coal. He also favored looser environmental regulations on air and water pollution, and increased mining and other commercial activities on public lands. Trump has said that he plans to withdraw the United States from the Paris Climate Accord, aimed at slowing global warming.

Even so, environmental leaders shared their visions of how the movement could continue—and even gain strength. Annie Leonard of Greenpeace said, "People around the country taking action are what's giving me hope right now."

As *Silent Spring* did in 1962, a book published in 1989 deeply influenced the environmental movement. It was called *The End of Nature*. Its author, environmentalist Bill McKibben, argued that human activity had changed the world so much that no place, not even the heart of a wilderness area, is untouched by humans. Air pollution and global warming have brought worldwide change, to say nothing of the many alterations humans have made to the world's landscapes, he said.

McKibben's point was that there is now no "pure" nature apart from humankind. For better or worse, the human species is changing the planet that is home to all species. More than 20 years later, a professor of global environmental politics named Paul Wapner published *Living Through the End of Naure: The Future of the American Environmental Movement*. He wrote:

" **Without nature, what *is* the American environmental movement? . . . [T]he end of nature, while fundamentally challenging to the movement, represents not a death knell but rather an opportunity.** "

Environmentalism is not dead, in other words. It is ready for new leaders, thinkers, scientists, educators, and activists to work toward the best possible future for the world that humans have made.

Solar panels are now being used
in the Mojave Desert.

ENVIRONMENTAL INSPIRATION

"You cannot get through a single day without having an impact on the world around you. What you do makes a difference, and you have to decide what kind of difference you want to make."

Jane Goodall, scientist known for studying wild chimpanzees

"A true conservationist . . . knows that the world is not given by his fathers, but borrowed from his children."

John James Audubon, known for his study and illustration of hundred of bird species

"We need the tonic of wildness—to wade sometimes in marshes where the bittern and the meadow-hen lurk, and hear the booming of the snipe; to smell the whispering sedge where only some wilder and more solitary fowl builds her nest, and the mink crawls with its belly close to the ground. At the same time that we are earnest to explore and learn all things, we require that all things be mysterious and unexplorable, that land and sea be infinitely wild. . . .We can never have enough of nature."

Henry David Thoreau, author of *Walden*

"Look deep into nature, and then you will understand everything better."

Albert Einstein, physicist who developed the theory of relativity

"Here is your country. Cherish these natural wonders, cherish the natural resources, cherish the history and romance as a sacred heritage, for your children and your children's children. Do not let selfish men or greedy interests skin your country of its beauty, its riches or its romance."

Theodore Roosevelt, the "conservationist president" of the U.S.

"It seems to me that the natural world is the greatest source of excitement; the greatest source of visual beauty; the greatest source of intellectual interest. It is the greatest source of so much in life that makes life worth living."

--David Attenborough, writer and documentarian of nature and wildlife

TIMELINE

1962—Rachel Carson's *Silent Spring* is published

1964—National Wilderness Act is passed

1968—National Wild and Scenic Rivers Act is passed

1969—More than 3 million gallons of oil leaked into the Pacific Ocean as a result of the Santa Barbara oil spill

1970—The First Earth Day march takes place on April 22

The year also sees the passage of the National Environmental Policy Act, the Clean Air Act, and the creation of the Environmental Protection Agency

1972—The Clean Water Act is passed

1973—The Endangered Species Act is passed

1980—Superfund begins to keep a list of all the toxic sites in the U.S.

1989—Bill McKibben's *The End of Nature* is published

1990—The Clean Air Act is strengthened

2000—The term *Anthropocene* is coined

2015—The Paris Climate Accord is signed by 195 nations

GLOSSARY

climate change—long-term change in Earth's climate, affecting temperature, rainfall, wind, and ocean currents

conservation—environmentalism that is focused on protecting or preserving land and wildlife

ecology—the interactions among living things and their environment, including what they eat, what eats them, and what competes with them

ecosystem—biological community of living things and their environment

environmental justice—the idea that all groups within society should be treated fairly and equally under environmental laws and policies, and that all should be involved in making environmental decisions

global warming—increase in Earth's average surface temperature since the late 18th century

greenhouse gas—an ingredient in the atmosphere, such as carbon dioxide or methane, that traps heat and makes Earth's temperature higher than it would be without the gas; greenhouse gases can be natural or human-made

pollution—harmful substances in air, water, or soil; or the act of introducing those substances

species—group of plants or animals that share common characteristics

toxic—poisonous or harmful to health

READ MORE

Archer, Jules. *To Save the Earth: The American Environmental Movement.* New York: Sky Pony Press, 2016.

Eboch, Chris. *Green Movement.* (Essential Library of Social Change). Minneapolis, Minn.: ABDO, 2013.

Rowell, Rebecca. *Rachel Carson Sparks the Environmental Movement.* Minneapolis, Minn.: ABDO, 2016.

CRITICAL THINKING QUESTIONS

1. What were some of the events that led to the rise of environmental awareness and activism in the 1960s and 1970s? Give examples from the text and link them with specific results.

2. List at least three methods of activism that have been used by environmentalists to achieve their goals. Give an example of each. What do you think are the strengths and weaknesses of each method, and why?

INTERNET SITES

Use FactHound to find internet sites related to this book.

Visit www.facthound.com

Just type in 9781543503883 and go.

ABOUT THE AUTHOR

Rebecca Stefoff has written books for young readers on many topics in science, technology, and history. She is the author of *Space Race: An Interactive Space Exploration Adventure*, the six-volume series Is It Science?, and the four-volume series Animal Behavior Revealed. Previous work on environmental history includes *The American Environmental Movement*. Stefoff lives in Portland, Oregon.

INDEX